Cute
BABY STUFF

10 Colorful Crochet Projects

LEISURE ARTS, INC. • Maumelle, Arkansas

Contents

LION BRAND® FEELS LIKE BUTTA BONUS BUNDLE®

Broomfield Hooded Baby Blanket

EASY

SIZE

About 29 x 29 in. (73.5 x 73.5 cm)

GAUGE

5 scallops = about 4 in. (10 cm).

BE SURE TO CHECK YOUR GAUGE.

MATERIALS

MEDIUM 4

Yarn (Medium)

Lion Brand® FEELS LIKE BUTTA BONUS BUNDLE® (Art. #123)

- ☐ #158 Lemon 2 balls
- ☐ Lion Brand® crochet hook size J-10 (6 mm)
- ☐ Lion Brand® large-eyed blunt needle

NOTES

1. Blanket is worked in 2 pieces: Blanket and Hood.
2. An edging is worked around the finished pieces, joining the Hood to the Blanket.

BLANKET

Ch 108.

Row 1: Work 2 dc in 3rd ch from hook (first scallop made), *sk next 2 ch, (sc, 2 dc) in next ch (scallop made); rep from * across to last 3 ch, sk next 2 ch, sc in last ch – you'll have 35 scallops at the end of this row.

Row 2: Ch 2, turn, 2 dc in first sc, *sk next 2 dc, (sc, 2 dc) in next sc; rep from * to last 2 dc, skip last 2 dc, sc in top of turning ch.

Rep Row 2 until piece measures about 29 in. (73.5 cm) from beg.

Fasten off.

HOOD

Ch 4.

Row 1: Work 2 dc in 4th ch from hook.

Row 2: Ch 3 (counts as dc in this row and in all following rows), turn, 2 dc in first dc, dc in next dc, 3 dc in top of beg ch – 7 dc at the end of this row.

Row 3: Ch 3, turn, dc in first dc, dc in each dc across to beg ch, 2 dc in top of beg ch – 9 dc at the end of this row.

Row 4: Ch 3, turn, 2 dc in first dc, dc in each dc across to beg ch, 3 dc in top of beg ch – 13 dc at the end of this row.

Rep Rows 3 and 4 until you have 49 dc.

Next Row (Hood Edging): Ch 2, turn, 2 dc in first dc, *sk next 2 dc, (sc, 2 dc) in next dc; rep from * to last 3 sts, skip next 2 dc, sc in top of beg ch.

Fasten off.

FINISHING

Edging

Pin Hood over one corner of Blanket, matching edges. Join yarn with a sl st to one corner of Blanket.

Round 1: Ch 2, 2 dc in same corner, work (sc, 2 dc) evenly spaced around entire outside edge of Blanket, working through both thicknesses when working over Hood at corner and taking care to work (sc, 2 dc) in each corner.

Fasten off.

Weave in ends.

LION BRAND® ICE CREAM® BIG SCOOP®

Springdale Granny Baby Afghan

EASY

SIZE

About 33½ x 33½ in. (85 x 85 cm)

GAUGE

1 Square = about 10½ x 10½ in. (26.5 x 26.5 cm).

BE SURE TO CHECK YOUR GAUGE.

MATERIALS

Yarn (Light) LIGHT 3

Lion Brand® ICE CREAM® BIG SCOOP® (Art. #922)

- ☐ #222 Mochi 1 ball
- ☐ Lion Brand® crochet hook size G-6 (4 mm)
- ☐ Lion Brand® large-eyed blunt needle

NOTES

1. 9 Squares are made separately, then sewn together to make the Afghan.
2. Each Square is worked in joined rnds with the RS always facing.
3. Have fun with the yarn colors! Arrange the different colored Squares any way you like.
4. For those who find a visual helpful, we've included a stitch diagram.

SQUARES *(Make 9)*

Ch 4; sl st in first ch to make a ring.

Rnd 1 (RS): Ch 5 (counts as dc, ch 2), 3 dc in ring, (ch 2, 3 dc in ring) twice, ch 2, 2 dc in ring; join with sl st in 3rd ch of beg ch-5 – you will have 12 dc and 4 ch-2 sps in this rnd.

Rnd 2: Sl st in first ch-2 sp, ch 5 (counts as dc, ch 2), 3 dc in same ch-2 sp, *ch 1, (3 dc, ch 2, 3 dc) in next ch-2 sp (corner made); rep from * 2 more times, ch 1, 2 dc again in first ch-2 sp; join with sl st in 3rd ch of beg ch-5 to complete first corner – 24 dc, 4 ch-1 sps, and 4 corner ch-2 sps (Two 3-dc groups and 1 ch-1 sp along each of 4 sides between corner ch-2 sps).

Rnd 3: Sl st in first corner ch-2 sp, ch 5 (counts as dc, ch 2), 3 dc in same corner ch-2 sp, *ch 1, 3 dc in next ch-1 sp, ch 1, (3 dc, ch 2, 3 dc) in next corner ch-2 sp; rep from * 2 more times, ch 1, 3 dc in next ch-1 sp, ch 1, 2 dc again in first ch-2 sp; join with sl st in 3rd ch of beg ch-5 – 36 dc, 8 ch-1 sps, and 4 corner ch-2 sps (Three 3-dc groups and 2 ch-1 sps along each of 4 sides between corner ch-2 sps).

Rnd 4: Sl st in first corner ch-2 sp, ch 5 (counts as dc, ch 2), 3 dc in same corner ch-2 sp, *(ch 1, 3 dc in next ch-1 sp) to next corner ch-2 sp, ch 1, (3 dc, ch 2, 3 dc) in corner ch-2 sp; rep from * 2 more times, (ch 1, 3 dc in next ch-1 sp) to first corner ch-2 sp, ch 1, 2 dc again in first ch-2 sp; join with sl st in 3rd ch of beg ch-5 – 48 dc, 12 ch-1 sps, and 4 corner ch-2 sps (Four 3-dc groups and 3 ch-1 sps along each of 4 sides between corner ch-2 sps).

Rnds 5-10: Rep Rnd 4 for 6 more times – 120 dc, 36 ch-1 sps, and 4 corner ch-2 sps (Ten 3-dc groups and 9 ch-1 sps along each of 4 sides between corner ch-2 sps) in Rnd 10.

Fasten off.

FINISHING

On a flat surface, arrange Squares into 3 rows of 3 Squares each.

Sew the Squares together to make the Afghan.

TIP: The easiest way to sew the Squares together is to sew 3 strips of 3 Squares each, then sew the strips together.

Border

From RS, join yarn with a sl st in any corner ch-2 sp.

Rnd 1 (RS): Ch 3 (counts as dc), work 4 more dc in same corner ch-2 sp, dc in each dc and ch-1 sp around, working 5 dc in each corner ch-2 sp; join with sl st in top of beg ch-3.

Rnd 2: Ch 3 (counts as dc), dc in each st around working 2 dc in each of the 3 dc at center of each 5-dc corner; join with sl st in top of beg ch-3.

Weave in ends.

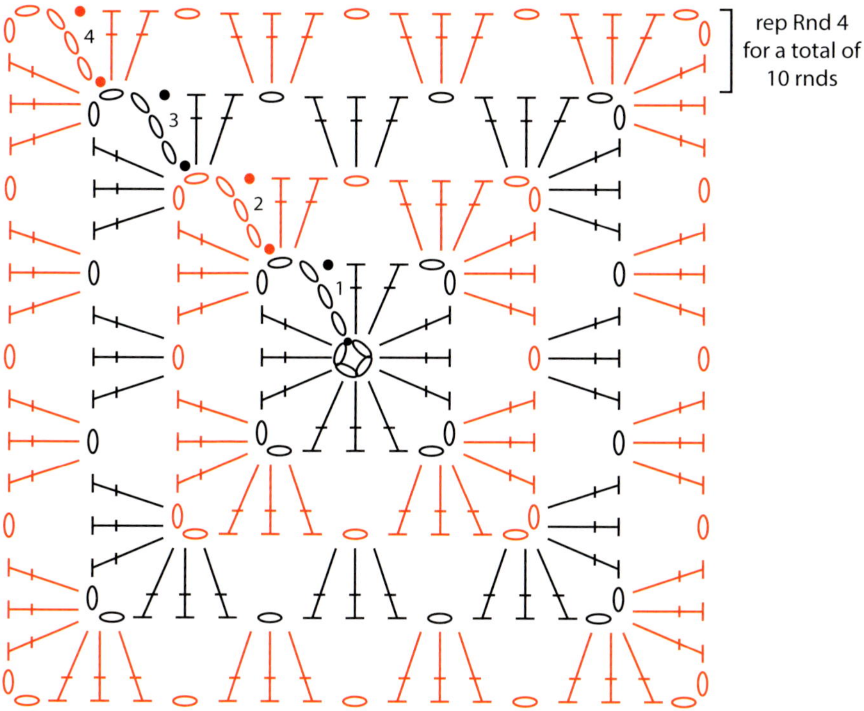

KEY

● = slip stitch (sl st)

⬭ = chain (ch)

Ŧ = double crochet (dc)

LION BRAND® ICE CREAM® BIG SCOOP®

Springville Circle Baby Afghan

EASY

SIZE

Finished Diameter:
About 41 in. (104 cm)

GAUGE

15 dc = about 4 in. (10 cm).

BE SURE TO CHECK YOUR GAUGE.

MATERIALS

LIGHT 3

Yarn (Light)

Lion Brand® ICE CREAM® BIG SCOOP® (Art. #922)

- ☐ #220 Parfait 1 ball
- ☐ Lion Brand® crochet hook size H-8 (5 mm)
- ☐ Lion Brand® stitch markers
- ☐ Lion Brand® large-eyed blunt needle

NOTES

1. Afghan is worked in one piece in joined rnds with RS always facing.
2. Increases are worked on each rnd to shape Afghan.
3. After the first 8 rnds are worked, stitch markers are placed for the increase locations, then increases are worked in each of the marked sts.

AFGHAN

Wrap yarn around index finger. Insert hook into ring on finger, yarn over and draw up a loop. Carefully slip ring from finger and work the sts of Rnd 1 into the ring.

Rnd 1 (RS): Ch 3 (counts as dc), work 11 dc into ring; join with sl st in top of beg ch-3 – you will have 12 dc in this rnd. Gently but firmly, pull tail to tighten center of ring.

Rnd 2: Ch 3 (counts as dc), dc in same st as joining sl st, work 2 dc in each st around; join with sl st in top of beg ch-3 – 24 dc.

Rnd 3: Ch 3 (counts as dc), 2 dc in next st, *dc in next st, 2 dc in next st; rep from * around; join with sl st in top of beg ch-3 – 36 dc.

Rnd 4: Ch 3 (counts as dc), dc in next st, 2 dc in next st, *dc in next 2 sts, 2 dc in next st; rep from * around; join with sl st in top of beg ch-3 – 48 dc.

Rnd 5: Ch 3 (counts as dc), dc in next 2 sts, 2 dc in next st, *dc in next 3 sts, 2 dc in next st; rep from * around; join with sl st in top of beg ch-3 – 60 dc.

Rnd 6: Ch 3 (counts as dc), dc in next 3 sts, 2 dc in next st, *dc in next 4 sts, 2 dc in next st; rep from * around; join with sl st in top of beg ch-3 – 72 dc.

Rnd 7: Ch 3 (counts as dc), dc in next 4 sts, 2 dc in next st, *dc in next 5 sts, 2 dc in next st; rep from * around; join with sl st in top of beg ch-3 – 84 dc.

Rnd 8: Ch 3 (counts as dc), dc in next 5 sts, 2 dc in next st, *dc in next 6 sts, 2 dc in next st; rep from * around; join with sl st in top of beg ch-3 – 96 dc.

Rnd 9: Ch 3 (counts as dc), dc in next 6 sts, 2 dc in next st and place a marker in last dc made, *dc in next 7 sts, 2 dc in next st and place a marker in last dc made; rep from * around; join with sl st in top of beg ch-3 – 108 dc.

Rnd 10: Ch 3 (counts as dc), *dc in each st to next marked st, 2 dc in marked st and move marker to last dc made; rep from * around; join with sl st in top of beg ch-3 – 120 dc.

Rnds 11-40: Rep Rnd 10 for 30 more times, increasing 12 dc in each rnd – 480 dc in Rnd 40.

Remove markers.

Rnd 41: Ch 1, sc in same st as joining sl st, sc in each remaining dc around; join with sl st in first sc.

Rnd 42: Ch 1, sl st in each st around; join with sl st in beg ch-1.

Fasten off.

FINISHING

Weave in ends.

LION BRAND® ICE CREAM® BIG SCOOP®

Crolla Baby Blankie

BASIC

SIZE

About 29 x 39 in. (73.5 x 99 cm)

GAUGE

14 half double crochet + 10 rows = about 4 in. (10 cm).

BE SURE TO CHECK YOUR GAUGE.

MATERIALS

Yarn (Light) LIGHT 3

Lion Brand® ICE CREAM® BIG (Art. #922)

- ☐ #209 Blue Moon 1 ball
- ☐ Lion Brand® crochet hook size G-6 (4 mm)
- ☐ Lion Brand® large-eyed blunt needle

NOTE

Blankie is worked in one piece in an easy stitch pattern.

BLANKIE

Ch 102.

Set Up Row: Hdc in 3rd ch from hook (2 skipped ch count as first hdc) and in each ch across – you'll have 101 sts.

Next Row: Ch 2 (counts as first hdc), turn, skip first hdc, hdc in each st across with the last hdc in top of turning ch.

Begin stitch pattern

Row 1: Ch 3 (counts as first hdc + ch 1), turn, skip next hdc, hdc in next st, *ch 1, skip next st, hdc in next st; rep from * across with the last hdc in top of turning ch.

Row 2: Ch 2 (counts as first hdc), turn, skip first hdc, hdc in each st and in each ch-1 space across, ending with the last hdc in top of turning ch.

Row 3: Ch 2 (counts as first hdc), turn, skip first hdc, hdc in each st across, ending with last hdc in top of turning ch.

Repeat Rows 1-3 until piece measures about 39 in. (99 cm) from beginning, end with Row 1 as the last row you work.

Fasten off.

FINISHING

Weave in ends.

LION BRAND® ICE CREAM® BIG SCOOP®

Hooded Blankie

EASY

SIZE

About 28 x 28 in. (71 x 71 cm)

GAUGE

6 scallops = about 5 in. (12.5 cm).

BE SURE TO CHECK YOUR GAUGE.

MATERIALS

Yarn (Light) LIGHT 3

Lion Brand® ICE CREAM® BIG SCOOP® (Art. #922)

- ☐ #215 Moon Mist 1 ball
- ☐ Lion Brand® crochet hook size I-9 (5.5 mm)
- ☐ Lion Brand® large-eyed blunt needle

NOTES

1. Blankie is worked in one piece.
2. Hood is worked separately and crocheted to Blankie.

BLANKIE

Ch 102.

Row 1: Work 2 dc in 3rd ch from hook (first scallop made), *sk next 2 ch, (sc, 2 dc) in next ch (scallop made); rep from * across to last 3 ch, sk next 2 ch, sc in last ch – 33 scallops at the end of this row.

Row 2: Ch 2, turn, 2 dc in first sc, *sk next 2 dc, (sc, 2 dc) in next sc; rep from * across, sc in top of turning ch.

Rep Row 2 until piece measures about 28 in. (71 cm) from beg.

Fasten off.

HOOD

Ch 4.

Row 1: Work 2 dc in 4th ch from hook.

Row 2: Ch 3 (counts as dc in this row and in all following rows), turn, 2 dc in first dc, dc in next dc, 3 dc in top of beg ch – 7 dc at the end of this row.

Row 3: Ch 3, turn, dc in first dc, dc in each dc across to beg ch, 2 dc in top of beg ch – 9 dc at the end of this row.

Row 4: Ch 3, turn, 2 dc in first dc, dc in each dc across to beg ch, 3 dc in top of beg ch – 13 dc at the end of this row.

Rep Rows 3 and 4 until there are 49 dc.

Next Row (Hood Edging): Ch 3, turn, 2 dc in first dc, *sk next 2 dc, (sc, 2 dc) in next dc; rep from * to last 3 sts, sk next 2 sts, sc in top of beg ch.

Fasten off.

FINISHING

Edging

From RS, pin Hood onto one corner of Blankie. Join yarn with a sl st at any corner of Blankie.

Round 1: Ch 2, 2 dc in same corner, work (sc, 2 dc) evenly spaced around entire outside edge of Blankie, working through both thicknesses when working over Hood at corner.
Note: Take care to work (sc, 2 dc) in each corner of Blankie.

Fasten off.

Weave in ends.

LION BRAND® BABY SOFT® BOUCLE

Cuddle Bunny Blankie

EASY

SIZE

About 15 in. (38 cm) long, not including ears

GAUGE

7 sc = about 4 in. (10 cm) with larger hook.

BE SURE TO CHECK YOUR GAUGE.

MATERIALS

BULKY 5

Yarn (Bulky)

Lion Brand® BABY SOFT® BOUCLE (Art. #918)

- ☐ #144 Lavender 1 ball
- ☐ Lion Brand® crochet hook size K-10.5 (6.5 mm)
- ☐ Lion Brand® crochet hook size N-13 (9 mm)
- ☐ Lion Brand® stitch markers
- ☐ Lion Brand® large-eyed blunt needle

Additional Materials

Small amount of black yarn for face

Small amount of fiberfill stuffing

NOTES

1. Blankie is worked in one piece. The Blankie is worked diagonally beginning at lower corner. The bunny head is worked in continuous rounds (spiral).
2. Increases and decreases are worked to shape the Blankie.
3. The bunny head is worked with a smaller hook so that stuffing will not show through spaces between stitches. Ears are worked directly onto sides of top of head. The eyes and nose are embroidered onto the head.
4. Do not leave small children unattended with the Blankie!

STITCH EXPLANATIONS

sc2tog (sc 2 sts together)
(Insert hook in next st and draw up a loop) twice, yarn over and draw through all 3 loops on hook – 1 st decreased.

sc3tog (sc 3 sts together)
(Insert hook in next st or ch-1 sp and draw up a loop) 3 times, yarn and draw through all 4 loops on hook – 2 sts decreased.

BLANKIE

With larger hook, ch 2.

Increase Section

Row 1: Work 2 sc in 2nd ch from hook.

Row 2: Ch 1, turn, 2 sc in first st, sc in next st – you will have 3 sc in this row.

Row 3: Ch 1, turn, 2 sc in first st, sc in next st, 2 sc in last st – 5 sc.

Row 4: Ch 1, turn, 2 sc in first st, sc in next st, ch 1, sk next st, sc in next st, 2 sc in last st – 6 sc and 1 ch-1 sp.

Row 5: Ch 1, turn, 2 sc in first st, sc in next st, ch 1, sk next st, sc in next ch-1 sp, ch 1, sk next st, sc in next st, 2 sc in last st – 7 sc and 2 ch-1 sps.

Row 6: Ch 1, turn, 2 sc in first st, sc in next st, ch 1, sk next st, sc in next ch-1 sp, sc in next st, sc in next ch-1 sp, ch 1, sk next st, sc in next st, 2 sc in last st – 9 sc and 2 ch-1 sps.

Rows 7-17: Ch 1, turn, 2 sc in first st, sc in next st, ch 1, sk next st, sc in next ch-1 sp, sc in each st to next ch-1 sp, sc in next ch-1 sp, ch 1, sk next st, sc in next st, 2 sc in last st – 31 sc and 2 ch-1 sps in Row 17.

Shape Paws

Row 18: Ch 15 for first paw, turn, sc in 2nd ch from hook and next 13 ch, 2 sc in next st, sc in next st, ch 1, sk next st, sc in next ch-1 sp, sc in each st to next ch-1 sp, sc in next ch-1 sp, ch 1, sk next st, sc in next st, 2 sc in last st – 47 sc and 2 ch-1 sps.

Row 19: Ch 15 for second paw, turn, sc in 2nd ch from hook and next 13 ch, **[**sc in each st to next ch-1 sp, ch 1, sk next ch-1 sp**]** twice, sc in each sc across – 61 sc and 2 ch-1 sps.

Row 20: Ch 1, turn, **[**sc in each st to next ch-1 sp, ch 1, sk next ch-1 sp**]** twice, sc in each st to end of row.

Row 21: Ch 1, turn, **[**sc in each st to next ch-1 sp, ch 1, sk next ch-1 sp**]** twice, sc in next 3 sts; leave rem sts unworked to complete first paw – 47 sc and 2 ch-1 sps.

Row 22: Ch 1, turn, **[**sc in each st to next ch-1 sp, ch 1, sk next ch-1 sp**]** twice, sc in next 3 sts; leave rem sts unworked to complete second paw – 33 sc and 2 ch-1 sps.

Decrease Section

Rows 23-27: Ch 1, turn, sc2tog, sc in next st, sc in next ch-1 sp, ch 1, sk next st, sc in each st to 1 st before next ch-1 sp, ch 1, sk next st, sc in next ch-1 sp, sc in next st, sc2tog – 23 sc and 2 ch-1 sps.

Row 28: Ch 1, turn, sc in first sc, sc3tog 8 times – 9 sc.

Row 29: Ch 1, turn, sc2tog, sc in next 5 sts, sc2tog – 7 sc.

Do not fasten off.

Bunny Head
Change to smaller hook.

Rnd 1: With smaller hook, ch 1, turn, working in front loops only, sc in each st across; turn to work in unworked loops along opposite side, sc in each unworked loop across – 14 sc.

Place a marker in last sc made for end of rnd. Move marker up as each rnd is completed.

Rnds 2-8: Do not turn, work in continuous rnds (spiral), sc in each st around.

Rnd 9: Sc2tog 7 times – 7 sc.

Stuff bunny head with a small amount of fiberfill.

Fasten off, leaving a long yarn tail.

Thread tail through sts of last rnd and pull to close top of head.

Knot securely.

Ears *(Make 2)*
With smaller hook, join yarn with a sl st at one side of top of head.

Row 1: Ch 15, sc in 2nd ch from hook and in each ch across, sl st in head – 14 sc.

Row 2: Turn, sc in each st to last 2 sts, sc2tog – 13 sc.

Row 3: Turn, sc2tog, sc in each st across, sl st in head – 12 sc.

Row 4: Turn, sc in each st to last 4 sts, sl st in each of last 4 sts – 8 sc.

Fasten off.

Rep on other side of head to make a second Ear.

FINISHING

With black yarn and following diagram, embroider straight st eyes, nose and mouth.

Tie each paw into a knot.

Weave in ends.

LION BRAND® BABY SOFT® BOUCLE

Covington Baby Afghan

EASY

SIZE

About 32 x 32 in. (81.5 x 81.5 cm)

GAUGE

Rnds 1-3 = about 4 x 4 in. (10 x 10 cm).

BE SURE TO CHECK YOUR GAUGE.

MATERIALS

BULKY 5

Yarn (Bulky)

Lion Brand® BABY SOFT® BOUCLE (Art. #918)

- ☐ #100 White 2 balls (A)
- ☐ #173 Sprout 1 ball (B)
- ☐ #157 Lemonade 1 ball (C)
- ☐ #144 Lavender 1 ball (D)
- ☐ #101 Ballet Pink 1 ball (E)
- ☐ Lion Brand® crochet hook size K-10.5 (6.5 mm)
- ☐ Lion Brand® large-eyed blunt needle

NOTE

Afghan is worked in one piece in joined and turned rnds.

AFGHAN

With A, ch 4; join with sl st in first ch to form a ring.

Rnd 1 (RS): Ch 3 (counts as first dc in this rnd and in all following rnds), 2 dc in ring, (ch 2, 3 dc in ring) 3 times, ch 2; join with sl st in top of beg ch – you will have 4 ch-2 sps and four 3-dc groups in this rnd.

Rnd 2: Turn, (sl st, ch 3, 2 dc, ch 2, 3 dc) in first ch-2 sp (first corner made), *(3 dc, ch 2, 3 dc) in next ch-2 sp (corner made); rep from * 2 more times; join with sl st in top of beg ch – 4 corner ch-2 sps and eight 3-dc groups (two 3-dc groups along each of 4 sides between corner ch-2 sps).

Fasten off.

Rnd 3 (RS): From RS, join B with sl st in first sp between 3-dc groups, ch 3, 2 dc in same sp, *(3 dc, ch 2, 3 dc) in next corner ch-2 sp, 3 dc in next sp between 3-dc groups; rep from * 2 more times, (3 dc, ch 2, 3 dc) in last corner ch-2 sp; join with sl st in top of beg ch – 4 corner ch-2 sps and twelve 3-dc groups (three 3-dc groups along each of 4 sides between corner ch-2 sps).

Rnd 4: Turn, (sl st, ch 3, 2 dc) in first sp between 3-dc groups, *(3 dc, ch 2, 3 dc) in next corner ch-2 sp, (3 dc in next sp between 3-dc groups) twice; rep from * 2 more times, (3 dc, ch 2, 3 dc) in next corner ch-2 sp, 3 dc in last sp between 3-dc groups; join with sl st in top of beg ch – 4 corner ch-2 sps and sixteen 3-dc groups (four 3-dc groups along each of 4 sides between corner ch-2 sps).

Rnds 5 and 6: Turn, (sl st, ch 3, 2 dc) in first sp between 3-dc groups, 3 dc in each sp between 3-dc groups to next corner ch-2 sp, *(3 dc, ch 2, 3 dc) in next corner ch-2 sp, 3 dc in each sp between 3-dc groups to next corner ch-2 sp; rep from * 2 more times, (3 dc, ch 2, 3 dc) in next corner ch-2 sp, 3 dc in each sp between 3-dc groups to end of rnd; join with sl st in top of beg ch – 4 corner ch-2 sps and twenty-four 3-dc groups (six 3-dc groups along each of 4 sides between corner ch-2 sps) at the end of Rnd 6.

Fasten off.

Rnd 7 (RS): From RS, join C with a sl st in first sp between 3-dc groups following any corner ch-2 sp, ch 3, 2 dc in same sp, 3 dc in each sp between 3-dc groups to next corner ch-2 sp, *(3 dc, ch 2, 3 dc) in next corner ch-2 sp, 3 dc in each sp between 3-dc groups to next corner ch-2 sp; rep from * 2 more times, (3 dc, ch 2, 3 dc) in next corner ch-2 sp; join with sl st in top of beg ch – 4 corner ch-2 sps and twenty-eight 3-dc groups (seven 3-dc groups along each of 4 sides between corner ch-2 sps).

Rnds 8-10: With C, rep Rnd 5 three times – 4 corner ch-2 sps and forty 3-dc groups (ten 3-dc groups along each of 4 sides between corner ch-2 sps) at the end of Rnd 10.

Fasten off.

Rnds 11-14: With D, rep Rnds 7-10 – 4 corner ch-2 sps and fifty-six 3-dc groups (fourteen 3-dc groups along each of 4 sides between corner ch-2 sps) at the end of Rnd 14.

Fasten off.

Rnds 15-18: With E, rep Rnds 7-10 – 4 corner ch-2 sps and seventy-two 3-dc groups (eighteen 3-dc groups along each of 4 sides between corner ch-2 sps) at the end of Rnd 18.

Fasten off.

Rnds 19 and 20: With A, rep Rnds 7 and 8 – 4 corner ch-2 sps and eighty 3-dc groups (twenty 3-dc groups along each of 4 sides between corner ch-2 sps) at the end of Rnd 20.

Fasten off.

Rnds 21 and 22: With B, rep Rnds 7 and 8 – 4 corner ch-2 sps and eighty-eight 3-dc groups (twenty-two 3-dc groups along each of 4 sides between corner ch-2 sps) at the end of Rnd 22.

Fasten off.

Rnds 23 and 24: With A, rep Rnds 7 and 8 – 4 corner ch-2 sps and ninety-six 3-dc groups (twenty-four 3-dc groups along each of 4 sides between corner ch-2 sps) at the end of Rnd 24.

Fasten off.

Rnd 25: With C, rep Rnd 7 – 4 corner ch-2 sps and one-hundred 3-dc groups (twenty-five 3-dc groups along each of 4 sides between corner ch-2 sps).

Fasten off.

Last Rnd: With A, rep Rnd 7 – 4 corner ch-2 sps and one-hundred and four 3-dc groups (twenty-six 3-dc groups along each of 4 sides between corner ch-2 sps).

Fasten off.

FINISHING

Weave in ends.

LION BRAND® BABY SOFT® BOUCLE - FEELS LIKE BUTTA

Polar Bear Baby Mat

EASY

SIZE

About 18 x 34 in. (45.5 x 86.5 cm)

GAUGE

13 hdc = about 4½ in. (11.5 cm).

BE SURE TO CHECK YOUR GAUGE.

MATERIALS

BULKY 5

Yarn (Bulky)

Lion Brand® BABY SOFT® BOUCLE (Art. #918)

- ☐ #100 White 6 balls (A)
- ☐ #101 Ballet Pink 1 ball (B)

MEDIUM 4

Yarn (Medium)

Lion Brand® FEELS LIKE BUTTA (Art. #215)

- ☐ #149 Pale Grey 1 ball (C)
- ☐ #100 White 2 balls (D)
- ☐ #153 Black 1 ball (E)
- ☐ Lion Brand® crochet hook size G-6 (4.25 mm)
- ☐ Lion Brand® stitch markers
- ☐ Lion Brand® large-eyed blunt needle

Additional Materials

Fiberfill stuffing

NOTES

1. Body, Head, Arms, Feet and other details are all worked separately, then sewn together to make the Mat.
2. Features are embroidered.
3. Head, Arms, and Feet are stuffed.

STITCH EXPLANATIONS

hdc2tog (hdc 2 sts together)
(Yarn over, insert hook in next st and draw up a loop) twice, yarn over and draw through all 5 loops on hook – 1 st decreased.

sc2tog (sc 2 sts together)
(Insert hook in next st and draw up a loop) twice, yarn over and draw through all 3 loops on hook – 1 st decreased.

BODY

NOTE: The top of the Body will be the back of the Head.

Beg at lower edge of body, with A, ch 52.

Row 1: Hdc in 3rd ch from hook (2 skipped ch do not count as st) and in each ch across – you will have 50 hdc in this row.

Rows 2 and 3: Ch 2 (does not count as a st), turn, 2 hdc in first st, hdc in each st to last st, 2 hdc in last st – 54 hdc in Row 3.

Row 4: Ch 2 (does not count as a st), turn, hdc in each st across.

Rep Row 4 until piece measures about 27 in. (68.5 cm) from beg.

Next 5 Rows: Ch 2 (does not count as a st), turn, (hdc2tog) twice, hdc in each st to last 4 sts, (hdc2tog) twice – 34 hdc in last row.

Fasten off.

HEAD

Beg at lower edge of head, with A, ch 56.

Row 1: Hdc in 3rd ch from hook (2 skipped ch do not count as st) and in each ch across – 54 hdc.

Row 2: Ch 2 (does not count as a st), turn, hdc in each st across.

Rep Row 2 until piece measures about 7 in. (18 cm) from beg.

Next 5 Rows: Ch 2 (does not count as a st), turn, (hdc2tog) twice, hdc in each st to last 4 sts, (hdc2tog) twice – 34 hdc in last row.

Fasten off.

CHEEKS *(Make 2)*

With B, ch 2.

Rnd 1: Work 6 sc in first ch; do not join, work in continuous rnds (spiral).

Place a marker in last sc made. Move marker up as each rnd is completed.

Rnd 2: Work 2 sc in each st around – 12 sc.

Rnd 3: *2 sc in next st, sc in next st; rep from * around – 18 sc.

Fasten off.

MUZZLE

With C, ch 18.

Row 1: Sc in 2nd ch from hook and in next 9 ch, hdc in next 6 ch, 4 hdc in last ch; working along opposite side of foundation ch, hdc in next 6 ch, sc in next 10 ch – 36 sts.

Row 2: Ch 1, turn, sc in first 12 sts, hdc in next 4 sts, 2 hdc in next st, 2 sc in each of next 2 sts, 2 hdc in next st, hdc in next 4 sts, sc in last 12 sts – 40 sts.

Row 3: Ch 1, turn, sc in first 14 sts, hdc in next 3 sts, 2 hdc in next st, hdc in next st, 2 sc in each of next 2 sts, hdc in next st, 2 hdc in next st, hdc in next 3 sts, sc in last 14 sts – 44 sts.

Row 4: Ch 1, turn, sc in first 16 sts, hdc in next st, 2 hdc in next st, hdc in next 3 sts, 2 sc in each of next 2 sts, hdc in next 3 sts, 2 hdc in next st, hdc in next st, sc in each of last 16 sts – 48 sts.

Row 5: Ch 1, turn, sc in first 18 sts, hdc in next 2 sts, 2 hdc in next st, hdc in next 2 sts, 2 hdc in each of next 2 sts, hdc in next 2 sts, 2 hdc in next st, hdc in next 2 sts, sc in last 18 sts – 52 sts.

Fasten off.

OUTER EARS *(Make 2)*

With A, ch 4.

Row 1: Sc in 2nd ch from hook and in each ch across – 3 sc.

Row 2: Ch 1, turn, 2 sc in first st, sc in next st, 2 sc in last st – 5 sc.

Row 3: Ch 1, turn, 2 sc in first st, sc in next 3 sts, 2 sc in last st – 7 sc.

Rows 4-7: Ch 1, turn, sc in each st across.

Row 8: Ch 1, turn, sc2tog, sc in next 3 sts, sc2tog – 5 sc.

Row 9: Ch 1, turn, sc2tog, sc in next st, sc2tog – 3 sc.

Fasten off.

INNER EARS *(Make 2)*

With C, ch 4.

Row 1: Sc in 2nd ch from hook and in each ch across – 3 sc.

Row 2: Ch 1, turn, 2 sc in first st, sc in next st, 2 sc in last st – 5 sc.

Rows 3-5: Ch 1, turn, sc in each st across.

Row 6: Ch 1, turn, sc2tog, sc in next st, sc2tog – 3 sc.

Fasten off.

TUMMY

With C, ch 14.

Rnd 1: Work 2 hdc in 3rd ch from hook (2 skipped ch do not count as a st), hdc in next 10 ch, 4 hdc in last ch; working along opposite side of foundation ch, hdc in next 10 ch, 2 sc in last ch – 28 sts.

Place a marker in last st made. Move marker up as each rnd is completed.

Rnd 2: Work 2 hdc in each of first 2 sts, hdc in next 10 sts, 2 hdc in each of next 4 sts, hdc in next 10 sts, 2 hdc in last 2 sts – 36 sts.

Rnd 3: (Hdc in next st, 2 hdc in next st) twice, hdc in next 12 sts, 2 hdc in next st, hdc in next st, 2 hdc in each of next 2 sts, hdc in next st, 2 hdc in next st, hdc in next 12 sts, 2 hdc in next st, hdc in last st and remove marker. Now work 2 hdc in next st, hdc in next st and mark hdc just made – 44 sts.

Rnd 4: 2 Hdc in first st, hdc in next st, 2 hdc in next st, hdc in next 2 sts, 2 hdc in next st, hdc in next 14 sts, 2 hdc in next st, hdc in next 2 sts, 2 hdc in each of next 2 sts, hdc in next 2 sts, 2 hdc in next st, hdc in next 14 sts, 2 hdc in next st, hdc in last st – 52 sts.

Rnd 5: (Hdc in first st, 2 hdc in next st) twice, hdc in next 3 sts, 2 hdc in next st, hdc in next 16 sts, 2 hdc in next st, hdc in next 3 sts, 2 hdc in each of next 2 sts, hdc in next 3 sts, 2 hdc in next st, hdc in next 16 sts, 2 hdc in next st, hdc in last st – 60 sts.

Rnd 6: Hdc in first 2 sts, (2 hdc in next st, hdc in next 2 sts) twice, 2 hdc in next st, hdc in next 18 sts, 2 hdc in next st, hdc in next 2 sts, 2 hdc in next st, hdc in next 4 sts, 2 hdc in next st, hdc in next 2 sts, 2 hdc in next st, hdc in next 18 sts, 2 hdc in next st, hdc in last 2 sts – 68 sts.

Rnd 7: 2 Hdc in first st, hdc in next 3 sts, 2 hdc in next st, hdc in next 5 sts, 2 hdc in next st, hdc in next 20 sts, 2 hdc in next st, hdc in next 5 sts, 2 hdc in each of next 2 sts, hdc in next 5 sts, 2 hdc in next st, hdc in next 20 sts, 2 hdc in next st, hdc in last 2 sts – 76 sts.

Rnd 8: Hdc in first 3 sts, 2 hdc in next st, hdc in next st, 2 hdc in next st, hdc in next 6 sts, 2 hdc in next st, hdc in next 22 sts, 2 hdc in next st, hdc in next 6 sts, 2 hdc in each of next 2 sts, hdc in next 6 sts, 2 hdc in next st, hdc in next 22 sts, 2 hdc in next st, hdc in last 2 sts – 84 sts.

Rnd 9: Hdc in first 4 sts, 2 hdc in next st, hdc in next st, 2 hdc in next st, hdc in next 7 sts, 2 hdc in next st, hdc in next 24 sts, 2 hdc in next st, hdc in next 7 sts, 2 hdc in each of next 2 sts, hdc in next 7 sts, 2 hdc in next st, hdc in next 24 sts, 2 hdc in next st, hdc in last 2 sts – 92 sts.

Rnd 10: Hdc in first 5 sts, 2 hdc in next st, hdc in next 3 sts, 2 hdc in next st, hdc in next 5 sts, 2 hdc in next st, hdc in next 26 sts, 2 hdc in next st, hdc in next 5 sts, 2 hdc in next st, hdc in next 6 sts, 2 hdc in next st, hdc in next 5 sts, 2 hdc in next st, hdc in next 26 sts, 2 hdc in next st, hdc in last 3 sts – 100 sts.

Rnd 11: Hdc in first 2 sts, 2 hdc in next st, hdc in next 4 sts, 2 hdc in next st, hdc in next 9 sts, 2 hdc in next st, hdc in next 28 sts, 2 hdc in next st, hdc in next 9 sts, 2 hdc in each of next 2 sts, hdc in next 9 sts, 2 hdc in next st, hdc in next 28 sts, 2 hdc in next st, hdc in last 3 sts – 108 sts.

Rnd 12: Hdc in first 6 sts, 2 hdc in next st, hdc in next st, 2 hdc in next st, hdc in next 10 sts, 2 hdc in next st, hdc in next 30 sts, 2 hdc in next st, hdc in next 10 sts, 2 hdc in each of next 2 sts, hdc in next 10 sts, 2 hdc in next st, hdc in next 30 sts, 2 hdc in next st, hdc in last 3 sts – 116 sts.

Rnd 13: Hdc in first 7 sts, 2 hdc in next st, hdc in next st, 2 hdc in next st, hdc in next 11 sts, 2 hdc in next st, hdc in next 32 sts, 2 hdc in next st, hdc in next 11 sts, 2 hdc in each of next 2 sts, hdc in next 11 sts, 2 hdc in next st, hdc in next 32 sts, 2 hdc in next st, hdc in last 3 sts – 124 sts.

Rnd 14: Hdc in first 8 sts, 2 hdc in next st, (hdc in next 4 sts, 2 hdc in next st) twice, hdc in next 42 sts, 2 hdc in next st, hdc in next 4 sts, 2 hdc in next st, hdc in next 8 sts, 2 hdc in next st, hdc in next 4 sts, 2 hdc in next st, hdc in next 42 sts, 2 hdc in last st – 132 sts.

Rnd 15: Hdc in first 4 sts, 2 hdc in next st, hdc in next 5 sts, hdc in next 13 sts, 2 hdc in next st, hdc in next 36 sts, 2 hdc in next st, hdc in next 13 sts, 2 hdc in each of next 2 sts, hdc in next 13 sts, 2 hdc in next st, hdc in next 36 sts, 2 hdc in next st, hdc in last 5 sts – 139 sts.

Rnd 16: Hdc in first 8 sts, 2 hdc in next st, hdc in next 6 sts, 2 hdc in next st, hdc in next 5 sts, 2 hdc in next st, hdc in next 46 sts, 2 hdc in next st, hdc in next 5 sts, 2 hdc in next st, hdc in next 10 sts, 2 hdc in next st, hdc in next 5 sts, 2 hdc in next st, hdc in next 46 sts, 2 hdc in last st – 147 sts.

Rnd 17: Hdc in first 5 sts, 2 hdc in next st, hdc in next 5 sts; leave remaining sts unworked – 148 sts.

Fasten off.

TUMMY SPOTS *(Make 7)*

With D, ch 8.

Row 1: Sc in 2nd ch from hook and in next ch, hdc in next 3 ch, sc in next ch, 2 sc in last ch; working along opposite side of foundation ch, sc in next ch, hdc in next 3 ch, sc in last 2 ch – 14 sts.

Fasten off.

ARMS *(Make 2)*

Beg at paw end of arm, with D, ch 2.

Rnd 1: Work 8 sc in first ch; do not join, work in continuous rnds (spiral).

Place marker in last sc made. Move marker up as each rnd is completed.

Rnd 2: Work 2 sc in each st around – 16 sc.

Rnd 3: *2 sc in next st, sc in next st; rep from * around – 24 sc.

Rnd 4: *2 sc in next st, sc in next 2 sts; rep from * around – 32 sc.

Rnd 5: *2 sc in next st, sc in next 3 sts; rep from * around – 40 sc.

Rnds 6-11: Sc in each st around.

Rnd 12: Sc in first 13 sts, sc2tog, (sc in next st, sc2tog) 4 times for thumb, sc in last 13 sts – 35 sc.

Rnds 13-60: Sc in each st around.

Rnd 61: *Sc2tog, sc in next 5 sts; rep from * around – 30 sc.

Rnd 62: *Sc2tog, sc in next 4 sts; rep from * around – 25 sc.

Fasten off.

FEET *(Make 2)*

Beg at toe end of foot, with D, ch 2.

Rnd 1: Work 8 sc in first ch; do not join, work in continuous rnds (spiral).

Place marker in last sc made. Move marker up as each rnd is completed.

Rnd 2: Work 2 sc in each st around – 16 sc.

Rnd 3: *2 sc in next st, sc in next st; rep from * around – 24 sc.

Rnd 4: *2 Sc in next st, sc in next 2 sts; rep from * around – 32 sc.

Rnd 5: *2 Sc in next st, sc in next 3 sts; rep from * around – 40 sc.

Rnd 6: *2 Sc in next st, sc in next 4 sts; rep from * around – 48 sc.

Rnds 7-26: Sc in each st around.

Rnd 27: (Sc2tog, sc in next 20 sts, sc2tog) twice – 44 sc.

Fasten off.

CLAWS *(Make 12)*

With C, ch 5.

Row 1: Sc in 2nd ch from hook, hdc in next 2 ch, (sc, ch 2, sc) in last ch; working along opposite side of foundation ch, hdc in next 2 ch, sc in last ch – 8 sts.

Fasten off.

FINISHING

Lay the Head onto a flat surface with the last row of Head at the top.

Referring to the diagram, sew the Muzzle and Cheeks to the Head.

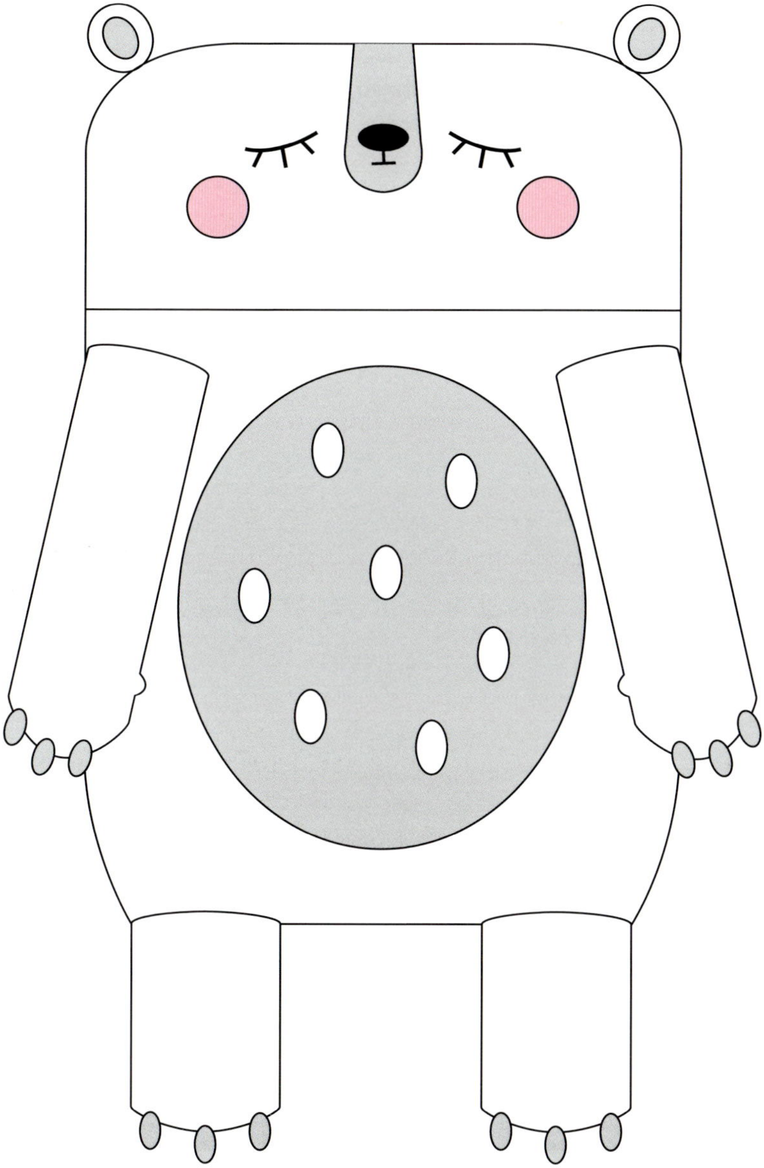

With E, embroider a straight stitch nose and mouth onto the Muzzle and sleeping eyes and lashes onto the Head.

Lay the Body with RS facing onto a flat surface, then lay the Head on top of the Body.

Sew side and top edges of Head to Body.

Sew the lower edge of the Head to the Body, loosely stuffing just before you finish sewing.

Sew Inner Ears to Outer Ears, then sew the Ears to the Head.

Sew Spots onto the Tummy, then sew the Tummy onto the Body.

Stuff Arms, firmly at thumbs, loosely for the rest of the Arms.

With thumbs pointing inward, sew Arms to Body.

Stuff Feet loosely and sew to Body.

Sew 3 Claws to the end of each Arm and Foot.

Weave in ends.

LION BRAND® BABYSOFT®

Pink V-Stitch Baby Throw

EASY

SIZE

33 x 36 in. (84 x 91.5 cm)

GAUGE

6 V-sts + 9 rows = 4 in. (10 cm) in pattern.

BE SURE TO CHECK YOUR GAUGE.

MATERIALS

LIGHT 3

Yarn (Light)

Lion Brand® BABYSOFT® (Art. #920)

- ☐ #220 Parfait Print 3 balls
- ☐ Lion Brand® crochet hook size G-6 (4.25 mm)
- ☐ Lion Brand® large-eyed blunt needle

Stitch Explanation

V-st: (Dc, ch 1, dc) all in indicated st.

THROW

Ch 148.

Row 1: (Dc, ch 1, dc) in 5th ch from hook (V-st made), *sk next 2 ch, V-st in next ch; rep from * across to last 2 ch, sk next ch, dc in last ch – 48 V-sts at the end of this row.

Rows 2-78: Ch 3, turn, V-st in ch-1 sp of each V-st across, dc in top of turning ch.

Do not fasten off.

FINISHING

Border

Rnd 1: Do not turn, work sc evenly spaced around entire outside edge of Throw, working 3 sc in each corner st; join with sl st in first sc.

Rnd 2: *Ch 2, sl st in 2nd ch from hook (picot made), sk next sc, sl st in next 2 sc; rep from * around.

NOTE: As you near the end of Rnd 2, count your remaining sts. If necessary, you can sl st in 1 or in 3 sc (instead of 2 sc), in order to end the rnd evenly.

Fasten off.

Weave in ends.

LION BRAND® ICE CREAM® BIG SCOOP®

Winsome Baby Afghan

EASY

SIZE

About 29 x 29 in. (73.5 x 73.5 cm)

GAUGE

One ripple = about 4 in. (10 cm) measured from peak to peak.

BE SURE TO CHECK YOUR GAUGE.

MATERIALS

Yarn (Light) LIGHT 3

Lion Brand® ICE CREAM® BIG SCOOP® (Art. #922)

- ☐ #221 Cake Batter 1 ball
- ☐ Lion Brand® crochet hook size G-6 (4 mm)
- ☐ Lion Brand® large-eyed blunt needle

NOTES

1. Afghan is worked in a ripple crochet pattern. The ripple pattern is easy to do, but it's important to remember that you may need to work several rows before the ripple pattern becomes clear.
2. The ripple pattern consists of alternating ch-3 sp "peaks" and skipped sp "valleys". Take care to keep the peaks and valleys of each row aligned. (3 Dc, ch 3, 3 dc) shells are worked into the ch-3 sp peaks, and a sp is skipped at valleys.

STITCH EXPLANATION

Cl (cluster)

Yarn over, insert hook in indicated ch or sp and draw up a loop, yarn over and draw through 2 loops on hook, *yarn over, insert hook in same ch or sp and draw up a loop, yarn over and draw through 2 loops on hook; rep from * once more, yarn over and draw through all loops on hook.

AFGHAN

Ch 164.

Row 1: Sc in 2nd ch from hook and in each ch across – 163 sts.

Row 2: Ch 3 (counts as first dc in this row and in all following rows) turn, sk first 3 sc, (3 dc in next sc, sk next 2 sc) 3 times, (3 dc, ch 3, 3 dc) in next sc, *(sk next 2 sc, 3 dc in next sc) twice, sk next 2 sc, Cl in next sc, sk next 4 sc, Cl in next sc, (sk next 2 sc, 3 dc in next sc) twice, sk next 2 sc, (3 dc, ch 3, 3 dc) in next sc; rep from * to last 12 sc, sk next 2 sc, (3 dc in next sc, sk next 2 sc) 3 times, dc in last sc – 7 ripples at the end of this row.

NOTE: Sts are now worked in sps between sts instead of into the tops of sts as usual.

Row 3: Ch 3, turn, sk sp between first dc and first 3-dc group, 3 dc in each of next 3 sps between 3-dc groups, (3 dc, ch 3, 3 dc) in next ch-3 sp, *3 dc in each of next 2 sps between 3-dc groups, Cl in next sp between 3-dc group and Cl, sk next sp between clusters, Cl in next sp between Cl and 3-dc group, 3 dc in each of next 2 sps between 3-dc groups, (3 dc, ch 3, 3 dc) in next ch-3 sp; rep from * to last four 3-dc groups, 3 dc in each of next 3 sps between 3-dc groups, dc in sp between last 3-dc group and turning ch.

Rep Row 3 until piece measures about 29 in. (73.5 cm) from beginning.

Fasten off.

FINISHING

Weave in ends.

General Instructions

ABBREVIATIONS

beg	begin(ning)
ch(s)	chain(s)
ch-sp(s)	chain space(s) previously made
cm	centimeters
dc	double crochet(s)
hdc	half double crochet(s)
hdc2tog	half double crochet 2 together
mm	millimeters
rem	remain(ing)
rep	repeat
Rnd(s)	round(s)
RS	right side
sc	single crochet(s)
sc2tog	single crochet 2 together
sc3tog	single crochet 3 together
sk	skip
sl st	slip stitch
sp(s)	space(s)
st(s)	stitch(es)
WS	wrong side

CROCHET TERMINOLOGY		
UNITED STATES		INTERNATIONAL
slip stitch (slip st)	=	single crochet (sc)
single crochet (sc)	=	double crochet (dc)
half double crochet (hdc)	=	half treble crochet (htr)
double crochet (dc)	=	treble crochet (tr)
treble crochet (tr)	=	double treble crochet (dtr)
double treble crochet (dtr)	=	triple treble crochet (ttr)
triple treble crochet (tr tr)	=	quadruple treble crochet (qtr)
skip	=	miss

CROCHET HOOKS	
U.S.	**Metric mm**
B-1	2.25
C-2	2.75
D-3	3.25
E-4	3.5
F-5	3.75
G-6	4
7	4.5
H-8	5
I-9	5.5
J-10	6
K-10½	6.5
L-11	8
M/N-13	9
N/P-15	10
P/Q	15
Q	16
S	19